Reycraft Books
55 Fifth Avenue
New York, NY 10003
Reycraftbooks.com

DEDICATED TO MY DAD. ALWAYS AN INSPIRATION. -A.W.

Reycraft Books is a trade imprint and trademark of Newmark Learning, LLC.

Educators and Librarians: Our books may be purchased in bulk for promotional, educational, or business use.
Please contact sales@reycraftbooks.com.

Library of Congress Control Number: 2021902246

ISBN: 978-1-4788-7380-8

Photo Credits: Front Cover, Jacket Front: Gandee Vasan/Getty Images; Title Page: Seregraff/Shutterstock; Page 2: Eastimages/Getty Images; Page 3A: Creatures/Alamy; Page 3B: knelson20/Shutterstock; Page 3C: Bell nipon/Shutterstock; Page 3D: Melinda Klein/Shutterstock; Page 3E: WilleeCole/Getty Images; Page 3F: nechaev-kon/Getty Images; Page 3G: B Christopher/Alamy; Page 3H: MPH Photos/Shutterstock; Page 3I: Anthony Wallbank/Alamy; Page 3J: Tammada/Shutterstock; Page 3K: Sarah2/Shutterstock; Page 3L: EugeneEdge/Shutterstock; Page 4: K_Thalhofer/Getty Images; Page 5A: Karoline Thalhofer/Alamy; Page 5B: mariait/Shutterstock; Page 6A: stilllifephotographer/Getty Images; Page 6B: stilllifephotographer/Getty Images; Page 7A: Erik Lam/Shutterstock; Page 7B: Iryna Kalamurza/Shutterstock; Page 7C: Javier Brosch/Shutterstock; Page 7D: cynoclub/Getty Images; Pages 7E, 7H, 16A, 16B, 16C, 17A, 28H, Back Cover, Jacket Back: GlobalP/Getty Images; Page 7F, 7G: Susan Schmitz/Shutterstock; Page 7I: Goldution/Shutterstock; Page 8A: vauvau/Getty Images; Page 8B: Tim Macpherson/Getty Images; Page 8C: Anna Hoychuk/Shutterstock; Page 8D: Tagwaran/Shutterstock; Page 9A: Kolapatha Saengbanchong/Getty Images; Page 9B: Silense/Getty Images; Page 10A: Maaike Glas/EyeEm/Getty Images; Page 10B: dimarik/Getty Images; Page 11: Lunja/Getty Images; Page 12A: Claus Lunau/Science Source; Pages 12B, 18F: Farlap/Alamy; Page 14: Anke Sauerwein/EyeEm/Getty Images; Page 15: Memitina/Getty Images; Page 17B: Bubuaom/Shutterstock; Page 17C: lkphotographers/Getty Images; Page 17D, 17E: jclegg/Getty Images; Page 18A: Andia/Getty Images; Page 18B: choicegraphx/Getty Images; Page 18C: Upyanose/Getty Images; Page 18D: Image Source/Getty Images; Page 18E: KateLeigh/Getty Images; Page 19A: picture alliance/Getty Images; Page 19B: Erik Isakson/Getty Images; Page 19C: Anna Kraynova/Alamy; Page 19D: monkeybusinessimages/Getty Images; Page 20: RichLegg/Getty Images; Page 21A: Philartphace/Getty Images; Page 21B: Popova Valeriya/Shutterstock; Page 21C: Bob Daemmrich/Alamy; Page 21D: BEHROUZ MEHRI/Getty Images; Pages 22, 23A: Aneta Jungerova/Shutterstock; Page 23B: Louise Murray/Science Source; Page 23C, 23D: Roger Hall/Science Source; Page 24A: sam74100/Getty Images; Page 24B: Deborah Kolb/Shutterstock; Page 24C: Oleksiy Rezin/Shutterstock; Page 24D: kzenon/Getty Images; Page 24E: Africa Studio/Shutterstock; Page 24F: THEPALMER/Getty Images; Page 25A: Roberto A Sanchez/Getty Images; Page 25B: Jen Wolf/Shutterstock; Page 25C: RichLegg/Getty Images; Page 25D: adogslifephoto/Getty Images; Page 25E: Javier Brosch/Alamy; Page 25F: Dakota Michelon/Shutterstock; Page 25G: tong patong/Shutterstock; Page 25H: Tara Lynn and Co/Shutterstock; Pages 26, 27A: Ksenia Raykova/Shutterstock; Page 27B: Double Brain/Shutterstock; Page 27C, Poster E: T.M.O.Pets/Alamy; Page 27D: Boris Zhitkov/Getty Images; Page 28A: Dorling Kindersley ltd/Alamy; Page 28B: Kuznetsov Alexey/Shutterstock; Page 28C: nickpo/Getty Images; Page 28D: Perky Pets/Alamy; Page 28E: cynoclub/Getty Images; Page 28F: Danita Delimont/Alamy; Page 28G: vauvau/Getty Images; Page 28I: vtls/Getty Images; Page 29A: Antagain/Getty Images; Page 29B, 29G, 29K, 29M: Eric Isselee/Shutterstock; Page 29C: alkir/Getty Images; Page 29D: frans lemmens/Alamy; Page 29E: Erik Lam/Getty Images; 29H: Dora Zett/Shutterstock; Page 29F: slowmotiongli/Getty Images; Page 29I: ClarkandCompany/Getty Images; Page 29J: TonicShooter/Getty Images; Page 29L: alkir/Getty Images; Pages 30, 31, Poster D: Seregraff/Getty Images; Page 32A, Back Flap: Provided by Phung Luu; Page 32B: VectorPlotnikoff/Shutterstock; Front Flap: Seregraff/Shutterstock; Inside Front Flap: JPRFPhotos/Shutterstock; Inside Back Flap: TrapezaStudio/Shutterstock; Inside Front Jacket A: ANNA TITOVA/Shutterstock; Inside Front Jacket B: Susan Schmitz/Shutterstock; Inside Front Jacket C: Monika Vosahlova/Shutterstock; Inside Front Jacket D: Luis Alvarez/Getty Images; Inside Back Jacket A, Inside Back Jacket B: Seregraff/Shutterstock; Inside Back Jacket C: SikorskiFotografie/Shutterstock; Inside Back Jacket D: Arthur Baensch/Getty Images; Book Spine, Jacket Spine: ClarkandCompany/Getty Images; Poster A: Scott Camazine/Alamy; Poster B: SensorSpot/Getty Images; Poster C: Africa Studio/Shutterstock

Illustration Credits: Pages 3, 7, 11, 13, 15, 17, 19, 21, 23 JuanbJuan Oliver; Page 30 Loren Mack

Printed in Dongguan, China. 8557/0421/17800

10 9 8 7 6 5 4 3 2 1

First Edition Hardcover published by Reycraft Books

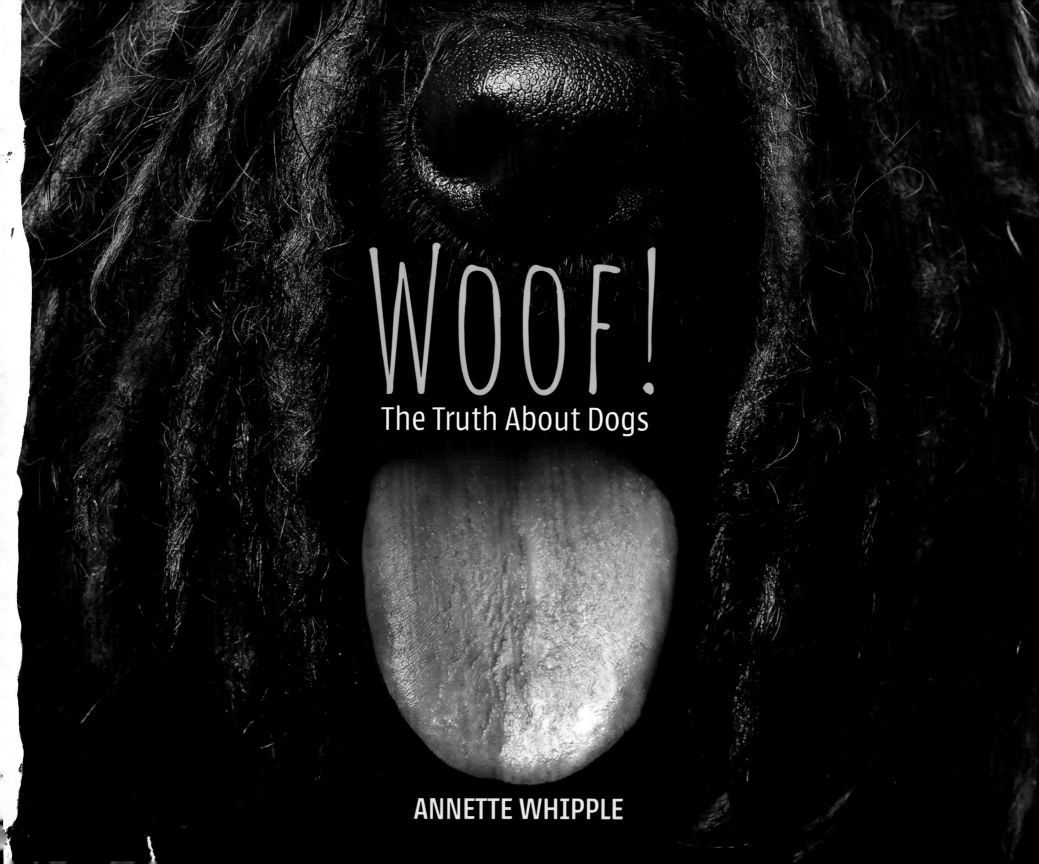

WOOF!
The Truth About Dogs

ANNETTE WHIPPLE

WHOSE TAIL IS THIS?

The wagging tail.

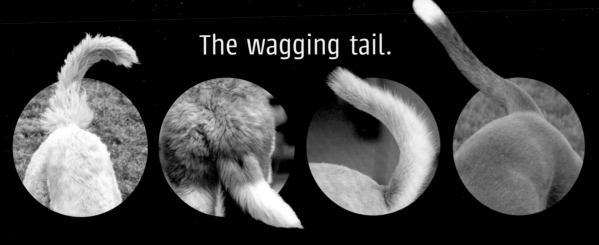

The sniffing snout.

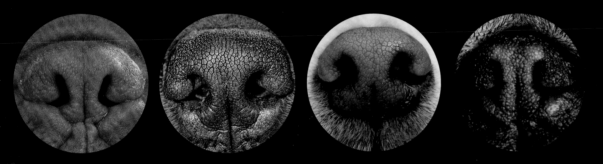

The happy bark.

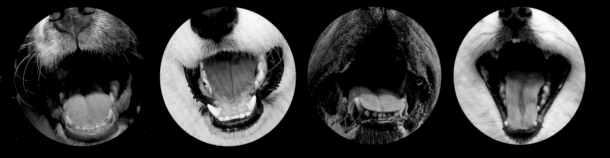

Dogs are the most popular pet in the world. But dogs chew our shoes, bark too loud, and slobber on everything. What makes these animals so loved? Let's find out.

Woof! Woof!

Can you help?

My friends live at your local animal shelter. They get lonely waiting for their fur-ever homes. They need volunteers like you to play with them.

Jack Russell Terrier

4

WHY ARE PUPPIES BORN WITH CLOSED EYES?

Jack Russell Terrier

Siberian Husky

A puppy and its siblings grow for just two months in their mother's womb. That's fast—too fast to fully develop. So, the newborn puppy's eyes don't open for almost two weeks. He doesn't have teeth at birth, either. And the puppy can't hear yet. He needs his mother for everything until he is about 8 weeks old. She feeds him and warms him. The mother even helps her newborn puppy go to the bathroom—and she cleans up by eating the mess!

Woof!
Woof!

Check out these new spots.
They just began appearing on my fur—like magic. About that same time, I opened my eyes and my hearing developed. Watch out world, here I come!

5

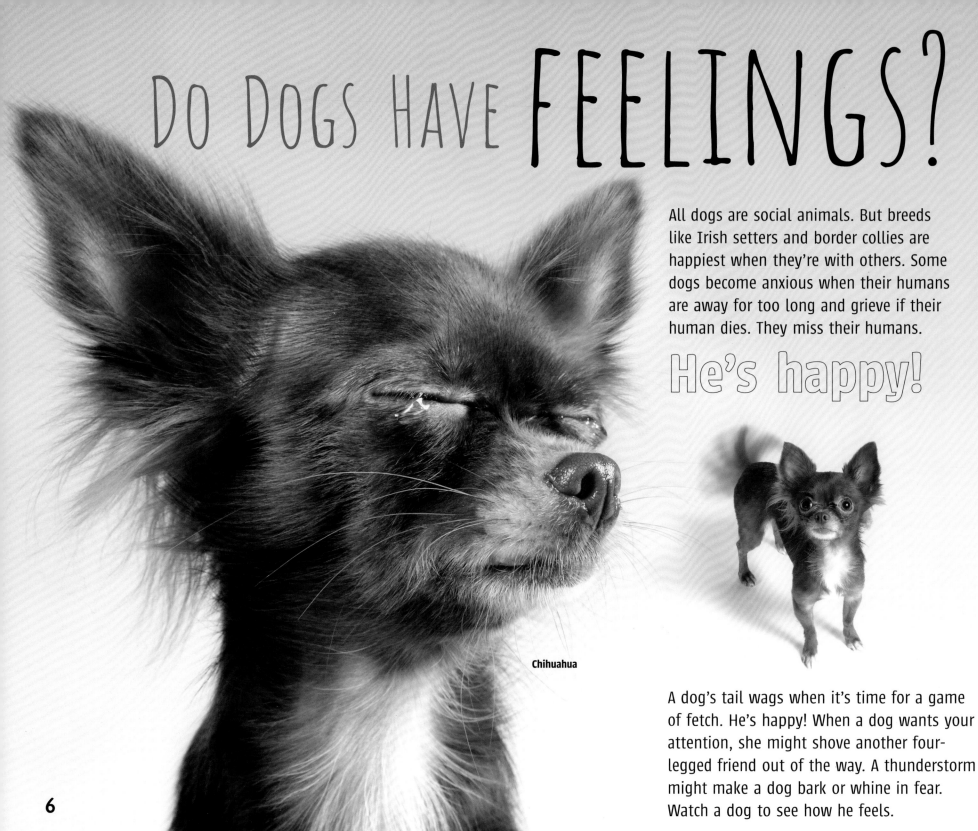

DO DOGS HAVE FEELINGS?

All dogs are social animals. But breeds like Irish setters and border collies are happiest when they're with others. Some dogs become anxious when their humans are away for too long and grieve if their human dies. They miss their humans.

He's happy!

Chihuahua

A dog's tail wags when it's time for a game of fetch. He's happy! When a dog wants your attention, she might shove another four-legged friend out of the way. A thunderstorm might make a dog bark or whine in fear. Watch a dog to see how he feels.

6

Relaxed

Happy

Submissive

Anxious

Scared

Angry

Defensive

Playful

Don't Bother Me!

Woof! Woof!

The itty-bitty human gets all the attention these days. I was jealous until I sniffed a smelly diaper. Now I understand, this baby is like a pup. It needs my help and protection.

Call me Nanny Dog.

7

How Do Dogs Communicate?

RUFF-RUFF

WOOF-WOOF

ARF-ARF

Mixed Breed

Dalmatian

Bark.

Mixed Breed

Growl.

Beagle

Whine.

Listen to a dog talk. Making sounds is one of the ways dogs communicate.

Does that bark mean he's hungry? Is a stranger in view? Does he want to go outside?

A dog's long, rising howl might show she misses you. Short, high-pitched yips reveal her excitement and curiosity.

Dogs also express themselves with their bodies. See that high-wagging tail? It shows friendliness and happiness. But a dog might be worried or afraid if his ears are back and his tail is down.

Dogs even invite others to play. They bend down on their front legs while keeping their tails high in the air. It's the play bow.

Dogs talk. We must look *and* listen to understand what they say.

Pomeranian

DOG TALK

Before a dog growls or snaps at annoying or unwanted actions, he typically tries to communicate that he wants to be left alone.

WARNING!

Watch for warning signs from a dog.

- turns head away or looks down
- shakes off the advance
- sniffs the ground
- licks lips
- lowers tail

STOP!

A stressed dog forces you to stop unwanted behavior.

- snaps
- growls
- bites

Basset Hound

DO DOGS SWEAT?

While dogs don't have many sweat glands, they do sweat. But sweat can't evaporate easily through their fur to cool them.

So, sweating cools dogs best in places where they don't have fur. Dogs' noses sweat. When air flows over a dog's wet nose, it dries the sweat and cools the dog. Dogs also sweat through their furless paw pads.

Your pooch pants when he gets hot. It's another way for him to cool his body. Panting lets body heat escape through the moisture of the tongue, mouth, and throat. Each exhaled breath keeps him cool as the wetness evaporates.

English Bulldog

Woof! Woof!

Hot dog!

I might want to eat one for lunch, but I don't want to be one. Can you get me some shade and extra water? And I wouldn't mind a dip in the pool. I can teach you how to doggie paddle.

11

WHY DO DOGS SNIFF EVERYTHING?

You can't meet a dog without getting sniffed. That's because dogs explore and discover their world through their noses.

Dogs smell thousands—possibly millions—of times better than humans. Their nostrils vacuum air inside their noses, which are full of scent receptors.

With their long noses, bloodhounds and basset hounds are often considered the super-sniffers of all dogs.

Bloodhound

Woof! Woof!

You can't hide it—
you smell.

I can't help but sniff you. It's how I know you are YOU. Your breath, armpits, and backside are full of smells. And your dirty socks? *Mmmm*, best smell ever.

13

WHY DO DOGS SMELL BUTTS?

Irish Wolfhound

Dogs learn all sorts of important information by sniffing another dog's butt. Right away, they know if the dog is male or female. They also learn what the other dog eats and its mood. It's all in their canine chemical communication.

Woof! Woof!

I skip smiles and handshakes.
One big whiff tells me you are pretty paw-some.

15

WHY DO DOGS CHEW SHOES?

Dalmatian Puppy

Dogs need exercise—both physical and mental. Without it, they get bored. And bored dogs entertain themselves. Chewing shoes, emptying hampers, and rifling through garbage cans are ways some dogs fight boredom.

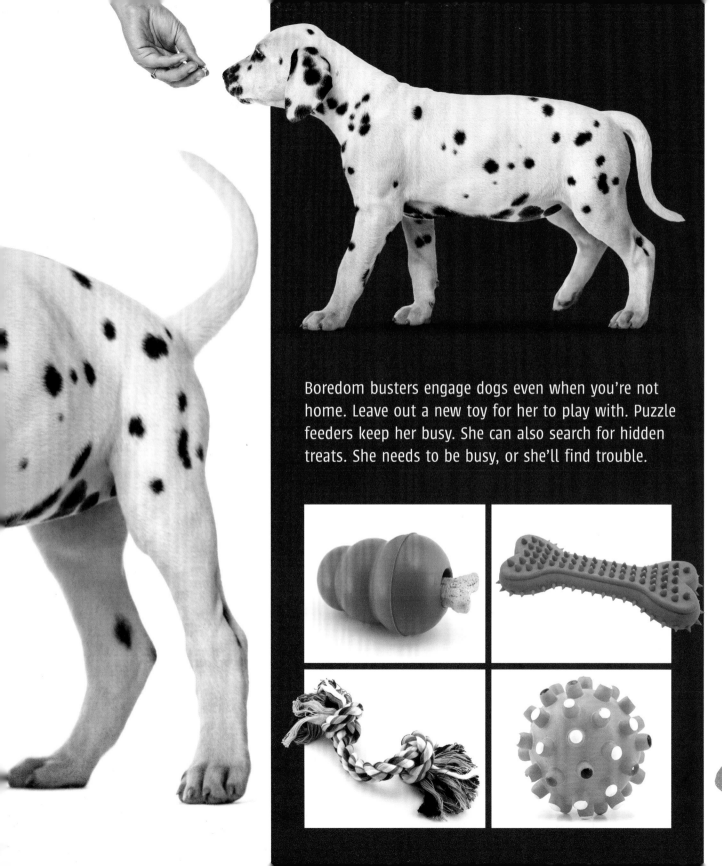

Boredom busters engage dogs even when you're not home. Leave out a new toy for her to play with. Puzzle feeders keep her busy. She can also search for hidden treats. She needs to be busy, or she'll find trouble.

Ruht-roh...
you're mad. I'm sorry. This time it wasn't because I was bored. My teeth are growing and hurt so much. Gnawing your shoe made them feel better.

17

How Do Dogs HELP PEOPLE?

German Shepherd

Labrador

Collie Spaniel

Doberman Pinscher

Border Collie

Australian Kelpie

Dog owners appreciate dogs' companionship. Not only do dogs give friendship and snuggles, they also relieve stress and reduce depression. Dogs are helpful in many other ways, too. Even without training, dogs have been known to alert families to fires and find help during emergencies. Many dogs protect families or businesses by warning their owners about strangers. Other dogs round up herds of sheep, cattle, or other animals to help farmers.

Service dogs live with their owners, but they aren't pets. They have jobs. Service dogs help people with disabilities or medical issues live better lives. They provide greater independence, security, and even joy to their owners. Handlers train dogs like poodles, golden retrievers, and mixed breeds to anticipate seizures or notice changes in blood sugar levels. Service dogs can listen for doorbells and crying babies or guide a person across a busy street. They also assist with daily needs. They open doors, turn lights off and on, and help a person transfer from a wheelchair to a bed.

Woof! Woof!

Take a look at this vest! My vest shows everyone I am a working dog. **I can play later**— right now my handler needs me.

Poodle

Cavachon

Maltese

Goldendoodle

19

How Do Dogs HELP THE POLICE AND MILITARY?

Other dogs work for the police or military. Handlers train intelligent dogs like Labrador retrievers and German shepherds to perform complicated tasks related to fighting crime.

Detection dogs use their incredible sense of smell to find specific scents. They sniff out drugs and explosives. They investigate possible arson fires and detect land mines. Patrol dogs stop dangerous suspects and hold them. Search and rescue dogs find lost people. They might search for a hiker in a forest, a skier buried in an avalanche, or someone trapped in an earthquake's rubble.

K-9
POLICE DOG

20

Labrador Retriever

German Shepherd

What's up, Pup?
We work hard in the K-9 unit. Our handlers expect full obedience—all day, every day. Are you up for the job?

21

Alaskan Malamute

Are Dogs
Just Tame Wolves?

Grey Wolf and Domestic Dog

It's easy to see how you might mistake an Alaskan malamute for a wolf. Scientists know today's dogs descend from wolves. The *Canidae* family includes dogs and wolves along with coyotes, jackals, foxes, and dingoes. They're all related. But wolves are wolves, and dogs are dogs. They're different.

Dogs are smaller than wolves—even big dogs like mastiffs and Great Danes. Dogs and wolves even live differently. The adults in a wolf pack raise pups together. Dog mothers rear their pups by themselves.

Then each puppy grows up to be a dog with...

A WAGGING TAIL,

A SNIFFING SNOUT,

AND A HAPPY BARK.

AND THAT'S THE TRUTH ABOUT DOGS!

Woof! Woof!

Let's get one thing straight.
As much as I like my dog food and an occasional critter, I could never eat like a wolf. One wolf can eat 20 pounds in a sitting!

Great Dane

Grey Wolf

How Can I HELP?

Kids Like You Can Help Dogs.

Be kind, because dogs treat others how they are treated.

Watch and listen to dogs' body language and barks.

Spay or neuter your dog to prevent overpopulation.

Black Pitbull Terrier

VOLUNTEER AT AN ANIMAL SHELTER.

Alaskan Mastiff

Jack Russell Terrier

Walk a dog.

Play with a dog.

Chocolate Labrador

Groom a dog.

Clean a dog's cage.

Bichon Frise

Read to a dog.

FUNDRAISE AND GIVE TO AN ANIMAL SHELTER.

Set up a lemonade stand or bake sale.

Sell treats or toys for dogs.

Buy dog food for shelter animals.

Collect old blankets and towels.

Donate approved toys or treats.

ADOPT.

Research dog breeds and mixed breeds.

Podenco Canario

Give a dog a fur-ever home.

Mixed Breed

Adopt Me!

How to
Meet
and Greet
a Dog

Mixed Breed

Always check with an owner before greeting a dog.

1. Let the dog greet you first. Be prepared to get sniffed.

2. If the dog is friendly, be friendly back. If the dog seems afraid or uninterested, ignore the dog. Watch for dog signals to know if your friendliness is welcomed or unwanted.

3. Be patient. It may take several meetings before a dog becomes friendly.

HOW **NOT** TO GREET YOUR DOG

DON'T
LEAN OVER HIM & STICK A HAND IN HIS FACE

DON'T
GRAB OR HUG HIM

DON'T
GRAB HIS HEAD AND KISS HIM

DON'T
STARE HIM IN THE EYE

DON'T
LEAN OVER HIM & STICK A HAND ON TOP OF HIS HEAD

DON'T
SHOUT IN HIS FACE

When you greet a dog, you might notice it has a wet nose. Why? The dog isn't sick. She's supposed to have a wet nose. Dogs lick their noses to understand their world better. She licks you. Then she licks her nose.

Sniff. Sniff.

Mucus inside the nose helps her to understand the scents she smells. Now she knows even more about you. A dog's nose is also unique. Just like you have a unique fingerprint, a dog has a one-of-a-kind noseprint.

Russian Toy Terrier

27

Which Dog?

Which Is the Largest Dog?	Which Is the Tallest Dog?	Which Is the Smallest Dog?

Mastiffs weigh about 230 pounds.

Irish wolfhounds stand about 32 inches tall.

Chihuahuas weigh less than 6 pounds and stand just 5–8 inches tall.

Other Large and Tall Dogs

Great Dane*

Newfoundland

Saint Bernard

Other Small Dogs

Toy American Eskimo

Coton de Tulear

Affenpinscher

*Though the breed is not known as the tallest, a Great Dane named Zeus measured an astonishing 44 inches in height and holds the record for the tallest dog.

Which Is the Fastest Dog?

Greyhounds can run about 45 miles per hour.

Other Fast Dogs

Saluki

Vizsla

Dalmatian

Jack Russell Terrier

Which Dogs Are Hairy?

Bearded Collie

Maltese

Yorkshire Terrier

Afghan Hound

Hungarian Puli

Which Dogs Are Hairless?

Xoloitzcuintli

Peruvian Inca Orchid

American Hairless Terrier

DIY Dog Tug Toy

Use old towels, blankets, or T-shirts to make chew and tug toys for the dogs in your life—or donate them to a local animal shelter.

Craft for Canines

Collect old clothes or towels. (Stains and holes are okay.) Wash them and then gather a group of friends to make dog toys. Make an appointment to deliver the tug-toy collection to your local animal shelter. Plan to stay and play with your new four-legged friends!

You'll Need:

- clean fabric (from fleece, T-shirts, or other material)
- scissors

What to Do:

❶ Cut four strips from the fabric. Each strip should be about 2 inches wide and 20–30 inches long.

❷ Stack the fabric together and tie a tight knot on one end.

❸ Spread fabric out to form a cross pattern.

❹ Hold the knot in your hand (or between your legs). Spread the fabric around your fist to form a cross pattern again.

❺ Move the top strip toward the bottom right. Move the bottom strip up toward the top left. Both should form small loops or arcs.

❻ Weave the left strip (from the original cross pattern) over the bottom strip's loop and then through the top strip's loop. Next, weave the right strip over the top strip's loop and then through the bottom strip's loop. Always go over and then through.

❼ Pull on the strips to tighten the newly formed square knot. (You should see a square begin to form with the four pieces of fabric.) Then pull some more to make a very tight knot.

❽ Repeat steps 4–7 until about 6 inches of fabric remain. Then tie a tight knot to finish the tug toy.

❾ Trim the ends of the fabric.

❿ Give the toy to a dog or donate it to an animal shelter.

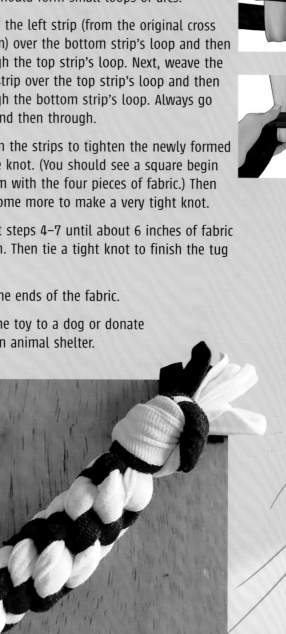

Glossary

blood sugar: the amount of glucose (sugar) in blood

canine: a dog, or animal related to dogs

develop: to grow

evaporate: change from a liquid into a gas

handler: a dog training expert

receptor: a cell in the body that receives and sends information to the brain

seizure: a sudden burst of electrical activity within the brain

social: friendly, or living with others

sweat gland: a tube in the skin where sweat is made

womb: the organ in the body where babies grow before they are born

Some Helpful Resources

www.akc.org

www.aspca.org

www.caninejournal.com

www.doghealth.com

www.dogster.com

pethelpful.com/dogs

www.petmd.com

www.rover.com/blog

ANNETTE WHIPPLE

Annette Whipple's first pet was a dog named Dog. Although she no longer has a dog, she enjoys visits with her furry friend Baxter. Annette's the author of fact-filled children's books including *Whooo Knew? The Truth About Owls.* When Annette's not reading or writing, you might find her baking for her family in Pennsylvania.